MANAGEMENT TIPS YOU ALREADY KNOW

(or maybe you don't)

Samuel J. Smith

Edited by Gary Greguras, Ph.D.

For information contact :

sjsokc@sbcglobal.net

Book and Cover design by Katelynn Smith.

Book Formatting by Meghan Castonguay.

ISBN: 9781096694625

First Edition: July 2018

10 9 8 7 6 5 4 3 2 1

CONTENTS

Introduction

I started as a home office life insurance underwriter in 1972 in Phoenix, Arizona and retired as the General Manager of a new life insurance company in Dublin, Ireland in 2013. At the height of my responsibilities I was in charge of 220 employees in 5 geographical locations (4 different states) and in 10 departments.

Each department had its own goals, priorities, and technological and personnel challenges. The same approach did not work in all departments. Learning by trial and error was the best way to address the challenges.

I learned management skills from seminars, books, observations, and experiences – both good and bad. Those skills constantly were being upgraded as technology and the work environment developed.

The purpose of this book is to share my management experiences with you in hopes that you will have a better understanding of the situations that you encounter. I believe that the contents have value for everyone, regardless of where one may be on the organizational chart.

Some of the chapters will be meaningful for managers only. If you are aspiring to get into management, you can use this as a training tool. Senior management may have forgotten what it was like in earlier positions. For these individuals this can act as a refresher.

I hope you enjoy reading this book. Ideally, you will take some of the points to heart and apply them to your own situation.

Acknowledgments

I would like to thank my editor, Dr. Gary Greguras. Even though he is my nephew, he was not shy in his criticism when appropriate. He used his experience in Singapore as a professor and author of Organizational Behavior and Human Resources.

I would like to thank my wife of 41 years and our four children. We journeyed together through my business career. I could not have acquired the knowledge, experience, confidence, and encouragement that resulted in this book without their devotion to me. I am eternally grateful.

MANAGEMENT PHILOSOPHY

Effective managers accomplish objectives through others.

You can delegate authority; you cannot delegate responsibility.

If you cannot do the little things correctly, why should you be trusted with the big things?

Better to be a smart ass than a dumb ass.

You cannot totally appreciate success until you experience failure.

Always give good news on Friday and bad news on Monday. Give bad news on Monday so the recipient does not have all weekend to dwell on it.

Address and eliminate excuses one at a time; eventually all excuses are gone.

Accuracy is critical.

You can do it right or you can do it over. I need it right

more that I need it now.

Wyatt Earp (Marshall, Tombstone, late 1800's): Fast is fine. Accuracy is final.

If the writing is on the wall, you should be writing on your resume.

If you cannot make your point within 5 minutes, you probably do not have one.

Successes fade with time; failures never do.

Do not blame everything on differences; sometimes others are just asses.

White Hat, Grey Hat, Black Hat

C olored hats? What does that have to do with anything? Colored hats are the political side of management.

Most of you reading this have a grey hat. It is the predominant choice.

Confusing? A Bell Curve is a good illustration of the distribution of hats. White hats are on the right side of the curve. Black hats are on the left side. Grey hats are in the middle.

You want to acquire a white hat if at all possible. Black hats are to be avoided. Those with grey hats are striving to acquire a white hat. Taking the wrong steps can downgrade a grey hat to black. Most new employees come in with a grey hat. There are some who start with a white hat. I will explain later.

Senior management dispenses white hats and black hats. Once a hat is given, it can be difficult to lose. Let us look at how you get a white or black hat. And then why it is important to know who among your peers and superiors have white hats or black hats.

If you have a white hat, you have access to the next level of management or even higher. Your ideas are given an audience. You are on the path to promotion. Your periodic reviews are pleasant and financially rewarding. Life is good.

There are two ways to get a white hat. One way is through superior performance. (e.g. or solved a previous expensive unsolvable problem.) Or if you are a recent hire and you bring skill sets to the organization that they have never had before. (The previous chief attorney lost a class action suit. You are the replacement. It is perceived that your skill sets are superior.)

In either case you may not be immediately awarded a white hat. But you are certainly on the list of people to watch for potential white hats. It may take more than one successful experience to acquire the hat.

The second method for acquiring a white hat is

having it gifted to you. Being the son-in-law of the CEO will get you a white hat. Having a good golf game, knowing how to find the bass in the fishing hole, or carrying yourself well at cocktail parties can win you a white hat. Race or gender also may play a key role in receiving a gifted white hat. Gifted white hats will usually outnumber earned white hats.

Black hats are awarded by any level of management above the recipient. Wearing a black hat usually means that someone would like to fire you but cannot for numerous reasons.

The three main reasons why black hats are still in the organization are as follows. You have alienated someone higher up the organizational chart. That person would like to get rid of you and may even consider you a threat. But someone even higher does not agree. The higher up is not in a position to gift you a white hat but is able to prevent you from being fired. I observed this many years ago when a manager was fired three weeks after his protector unexpectedly passed away. It came as no surprise to anyone.

The second main reason for a black hat remaining in the organization is that the organization has failed to purge itself of an employee who displayed incompetence early in one's career and never improved. The employee continued to work, continued to fail, but nothing was done. Now you have an incompetent employee that has time with the company, and time in their position thereby making it almost impossible to use incompetency as a reason, given the employee has been performing the same tasks for a period of time. Additionally, age, time with the company, gender and race can be factors in the decision to not fire the person.

The third main reason is that an employee is a close associate of someone who obviously has a black hat or was fired. Guilt by association. It happens all the time. It takes time to overcome that black hat.

Other reasons are usually trivial – do not like the way they dress, do not like the tone or volume of their voices, do not like the way they treat their coworkers, spends too much time on the phone, and so on.

Obviously, you want to associate yourself with employees who are wearing white hats. It is important to be able to identify who they are. The grapevine will tell you who the gifted white hats are. Determining those with white hats that earned them will take time and observation.

Position and title are good indicators of the person's potential of having a white hat. The Department Head would seem to have a white hat. But if they have been in the same position and same title for many years, they have not earned a white hat. But they may have been gifted a white hat.

Those employees with white hats or are on track for a white hat get invited to management meetings. One of the benefits of having a white hat is there is an audience for your ideas. Meetings are usually called to resolve problems and problems are resolved by new ideas. So if you start getting invited to the meetings, be sure that you go prepared. Do not offer an idea to try to impress if you have not thought it all the way through. Impressions can go two ways.

Black and grey hats can also get invited to meetings if they have a specialized skill set that is applicable to the problem being addressed. Do not try to impress others by criticizing the black hat's suggestions. Unless you have something positive to offer, just observe.

Do not be surprised if their opinion of their slice of the problem is solicited and then they are promptly dismissed from the balance of the meeting. And if you are invited to leave prior to the conclusion of the meeting, it is a fair indicator that you crossed a line somewhere. Note who asks you to leave so you can evaluate if that person has a white hat. You may need to avoid this person in the future.

I never got a white hat. I would like to think that I had several business accomplishments that would have warranted a white hat. I know several persons with lesser accomplishments that got white hats. I know why I did not get a white hat. With my personal management style, it was not to be. But the company was far better off for my being there. And for that, I have no regrets.

Protect Your Boss

D o you like or hate your boss? It does not matter. Your approach to protecting your boss should be the same regardless of your opinion. Your boss can make or break you. And will break you if you present yourself as a foe.

It is easy to protect a boss you like. Protecting them can become a challenge if you are not that enamoured with them or their performance. Suck it up; you have to do it.

The first step is to determine if your boss has a white, grey, or black hat. Review the chapter on this topic before proceeding.

If your boss has a white hat, it is beneficial for you to protect them. They are potentially on the way up the corporate ladder and they may take you along for the ride. If your boss has their white hat because of a relationship that they have with someone higher in the organization, your protective actions may come to the attention of that person. There are benefits for you if that occurs.

Those higher up will be even more appreciative of your actions if they are aware, as you are, that your boss does not have the skill sets required for this or any other position he might hold. Rarely will all three of you be aware of the truth.

A boss with a grey hat is eligible for promotion. As mentioned previously, their promotion usually only happens based on performance. If and when they are promoted, someone needs to take their place. If you are a strong supporter of your boss, her recommendation may be for you to replace her. That was how I got one of my promotions. My boss thought he had a black hat but I believed it was just dark grey. He recommended that I replace him. Even if he had not recommended me, I would like to think that my performance would have been sufficient to at least have been considered for the position.

Black hat bosses require special handling. You do not want to be viewed as joined at the hip with a black hat boss. This could win you your own black hat inadvertently.

If your boss has a black hat secondary to poor

performance, supporting your boss and trying to make him successful will be viewed as loyalty to the company. You are doing your best from the company's viewpoint to minimize a bad situation. Loyalty to the company is recognized and may be rewarded by a transfer to another department. This is exactly what happened to me. The president of the company recognized the bad situation I was in and moved me to a better situation. This opened up new opportunities for me.

Before I get into how to support your boss, there are two additional points that deserve attention. First, you need to determine who your boss's friends and enemies are. Depending on your relationship, your boss may be your best source for this information.

Do not ask your boss for this information. If this information is not readily volunteered, then you need to count on your keen sense of observation. How do the white hats treat your boss? Do they go to lunch together? Do they socialize out of the office? And your primary source is the office grapevine. While the grapevine is not always reliable, it may be the only source that you have.

Employees with longevity with the company have the benefit of knowing the history of the company and its people. They may know how your boss got his current position, who was beaten out during the promotion process, and how people higher up in the organizational chart achieved their positions. Be sure to filter the information that they provide. It is usually easy to detect resentment as the history is shared with you. Be careful acting on what may be a slanted opinion of the actual facts. Try to corroborate with another source.

Second, you need to determine where you are in the eyes of your boss. Are you viewed as an ally or a threat? Will they throw you under the bus to save their own skins or are you in this together? Knowing where you are with your boss will make a difference in how you support and protect your boss. Protecting your boss is still important regardless of your opinion of your boss and his opinion of you.

How to protect your boss is a combination of two things: information and communication. You need to provide your boss with regular and irregular contacts. Regular contacts are the easiest to establish. Make sure that you have access to the required information. Communicate it to your boss in a format and at a time that are acceptable. The only way to determine the format and timing to share the information is to have a direct discussion with your boss as to his expectations

Be prepared to provide input during this discussion. This may look like a golden opportunity to discredit the boss you do not like, but remember that you may inherit your boss's position and then you will inherit this flawed report. Or the boss is successful in showing that you are the fault with the report. There really is no down side to doing it correctly. If you are called upon to present the report to senior management, would you be comfortable doing so? Your goal should be to take ownership of the report.

Irregular contacts can be a little trickier and here is where you may struggle protecting the boss you may not particularly like. The format of the contacts should again be discussed with your boss. The difference is that you control the timing.

For projects that are assigned to you by your boss, you need to discuss what the expectations are regarding regular updates of the project. Irregular contacts are those where the project has hit a bump in the road, a new problem, or an unexpected delay. What does the boss want to know and when is it needed to be known? Have your boss give you guidance.

If exceptions only need to be reported during regular contacts, there is a situation where you need to violate that guidance. If the boss has regularly scheduled meetings with senior management, find out when those meetings take place. Prior to the meeting make your boss aware of any exceptions to your projects that have occurred since your last regular contact. There is nothing worse than being in a meeting and another attendee knows more about the problems of your projects than your boss does. Do not give your boss's peer group the opportunity to provide embarrassing commentary during the meeting.

There may be times when your boss's superiors assign you projects. Even though your boss was skipped in the assignment process, it is your responsibility to inform your boss of the project, who gave it to you, what are the expectations and how that project is progressing. It is protecting your boss and protecting yourself. I would hate to try to explain to my boss that I failed on his project because I was working on another project that he knew nothing about. And as a side note, if senior management assigns you projects without going through your boss, that should give you some insight as to where both of you stand at least with the senior officer who assigned the project.

Remember how you did not keep your boss informed and he was embarrassed at a meeting? He was embarrassed because other bosses were protected by their people. They were informed of what was going on in your department. You need to do the same for your boss. Keep your boss informed of what is going on in other departments.

Protecting your boss can be a challenge. And at times it can be a distasteful process. Overall, it is to your advantage to protect your boss.

E-Mail Etiquette

E -mail is a terrific communication tool. It allows you to communicate your exact thoughts and gives you the opportunity to edit those thoughts prior to distribution. It allows you to pick your audience. It gives that audience immediate access to what you are conveying. It lets your audience know who in your peer/superior group is also receiving the message.

When should I use e-mail? If more than one person needs to have access to the same information. If instructions need to be detailed for someone to follow and implement. If a record of what was discussed, decided, or suggested needs to be retained for future reference.

When should I not use e-mail? If something needs to be done immediately, then a phone call or personal visit is likely more effective and efficient. It is OK to follow up the conversation with an e-mail to summarize key points. Taking the approach of initially sending an e-mail and assuming that the appropriate action will happen are grave errors (see chapter on The Dumb-Tough Rule). Getting the problem off your desk may not be the solution. And e-mail is never the means to take personal shots at fellow employees. If you cannot say something nice, do not say it. (See chapter on Murder by Memo for those situations.)

Examining the various components of the e-mail is important. Understanding how each piece properly plays a role in your communication is critical.

The To: Line – The tendency is to put the name of everyone that you want to read the e-mail on this line. That is not correct. The To: line should only contain the names of those people that you expect to either take action, that you expect a response from, or to whom you are responding. If you want Bill to take a particular action and you want Mary to know that you have given this directive, then the e-mail should be sent to Bill and Mary copied.

The cc: Line – In the example above, you put Mary on the cc: line because you want Mary to know that you gave Bill a directive. Maybe Mary told you to do something and you are passing the directive on to Bill. Now Mary knows that you are not expecting a response from her. And more importantly, Mary knows when she opens the e-mail that if she currently does not have time, she does not have to read it. If numerous people need to know that a specific action is happening, then include them on the cc: line. But do not put the entire hierarchy of the company on this line. You need to determine what the accepted lines of communication are for your company. Some superiors want to control all communications that are going up the chain of command and they may not look kindly on you directly communicating with their superiors.

The bcc: Line – Be careful using this line. This line is almost exclusively political. You are wanting to share with Person A the content of your e-mail but do not want to tell another person(s) that Person A knows. The key is knowing if Person A is a true ally and will not forward your email to others. The bcc: line will normally only be used when you are in a Murder By Memo environment – which is described later in this book.

Subject Line – This line is mishandled more times than not. First of all the subject of your e-mail should be as short as possible. At the same time it needs to be clear. When the recipient gets the e-mail, he should know by the subject line the primary topic that is being addressed. Keep in mind that it is not unusual for a manager to receive multiple e-mails in a day. Whom it is from and what the subject says are the only two clues that help drive the priority in which e-mails are read.

As previously stated, one of the reasons for sending an e-mail is to establish a record for future reference. Have you ever had the situation of "oh, yes, I read that e-mail and have it somewhere but I can't find it right now."? When creating an e-mail, the subject line may be your primary clue to filing and finding the e-mail. If you receive an e-mail that you need to keep for future reference and the subject line is not clear, forward the e-mail to yourself and change the subject line to fit your filing needs. If necessary, it would include sending it to yourself twice and filing it in two separate folders. This may help ensure that you can find the e-mail when you need it.

Putting part of your message text in the subject line is only acceptable if your e-mail is a personal e-mail and not business oriented. "Break room at 10:30?", "lunch in the cafeteria?" – these types of e-mails are OK, but "the system will be down for" and then finish the conversation in the text of the e-mail is not acceptable. When you do this, you are forcing the recipients to rename the e-mail if they elect to save it for future reference. There may be persons higher in the organizational chart who will not appreciate but will remember this.

Body of the Message – I am sure that you are aware of the Five W's – who, what, why, where, and when. The "who" has already been defined by the To: line of the e-mail. The "what" has been suggested by a clear concise Subject line. Now it is time to expand on the "what".

The first sentence must specifically state the purpose of

the e-mail. You have gotten the attention of the recipient to open the e-mail. Now you need to give them a reason to keep reading. Especially those folks that you included on the cc: line. The creation of this sentence also gives you the opportunity to ensure that there is only one purpose to the e-mail. If there are multiple purposes, then you need to send multiple e-mails. There should only be one purpose for the e-mail.

If you really want to discourage the reader from reading the rest of your e-mail, then make the e-mail really long. Staring at a multiple paragraph, single spaced, margin to margin text will create one of two reactions – either not read at all or just scanned.

The longer the text, the greater the risk of error by the author (and reader) of the e-mail. If you leave out a word, "you will not do" becomes "you will do" will create problems. You may make contradictory points. You may convert a single purpose e-mail into multiple purposes. None of these have favorable results.

Know your audience. If your entire To: line and cc: line are technical people, than it is OK to use technical terms and abbreviations. If not, then the opening paragraph of your text should be as generic as possible. State the purpose of the e-mail as to what needs to be done and why in the first paragraph. And possibly the most critical, state when you expect a response or implementation of the requested action. Never put this information at the end of your e-mail as your only indication. If you want to repeat it at the end to reinforce the time constraints, that is fine.

Now you can get into the technical details of what needs to be done.

In most cases the persons listed on the cc: line are persons who are higher up the organizational chart than yourself. You included them because you want them to read at least a portion of what is being presented. Presenting a very long e-mail, which may be necessary, may put them in the not read at all or scan category. There are two ways to help avoid this.

If you have a long, detailed explanation that is really meant for the persons on the To: line, put that explanation in a separate document and attach it to the e-mail. Then the cc: folks have the option of whether they want to look at it or not. But they are able to read the short generic text that you provided for them.

The second option is to again present your short generic text and then number your detailed technical text below it. Numbering does three things. It alerts the casual reader that they probably do not have to read it. It enables you to provide your thoughts in a logical manner and helps keeping you from presenting contradictions. Rambling jumbled text can result in embarrassment. And when the persons on the To: line respond with questions or comments, they can direct you to their area of concern – "I don't understand what you meant on Number 7"; "I do not think number 3 will work."

You are almost ready to hit the send button. Not quite yet. Read the body of your text out loud to yourself. While spell check can spell words correctly, it does not always use the word you had intended. It would not hurt to review your To: and cc: lines to make sure you did not leave someone out or included someone that does not need to be on the list. Nothing is more frustrating for senior management than to be included on an e-mail that has absolutely nothing to do with them.

Replying to E-mail – You were on the original To: line. You have a question. Reply only to the originator of the e-mail. Do not hit Reply All or copy the others on the To: line. And there is a reason for this. Either you didn't understand what was presented to you or what was presented was not clear and concise. Either way at least one of you is going to appear stupid. Keep that between you and the originator. If possible, do not send an e-mail; call them and have a discussion.

When you have completed the task or action that was assigned to you, hit the Reply All button. Like the original e-mail you received, keep the same subject line and keep the text short and concise and announce the implementation date/time.

REMEMBER - E-mails are like birthday gifts. Once sent you are no longer the owner. They can be re-gifted (see chapter on Murder by Memo). E-mails are a picture of you and give you an opportunity to present yourself to others who have never met or dealt with you. Do e-mails correctly and make a good impression, be effective, and be efficient.

Meeting Protocols

"I have spent all day in meetings. I cannot get anything productive done." If it seems like you spend most of your working day in meetings, then there is something wrong. You are being invited to more meetings than you need to attend. The meetings are not accomplishing their intended purpose with a result of having to repeat meetings to discuss the same topic. The meeting that should last 20 minutes is lasting an hour.

Meetings can be the biggest waste of everyone's time if they are not approached properly. If you are not the person arranging the meeting, you are at the mercy of the person who is. You cannot control what meetings may require your presence. The meeting leader controls how long the meeting lasts. They control what, if anything, is accomplished. It is your duty to make your meetings the most productive when you have control over the factors that make a good meeting.

One factor that dooms a meeting is too many people at the meeting. I was excited when I was invited to my first meeting. My personal goal was to say something, either introduce a little-known fact or express an opinion. I needed to add value – at least from my perspective – to ensure that I would be invited to subsequent meetings. If you have several people with the same attitude, you will end up addressing unnecessary subjects. When unnecessary topics are discussed there is a possibility that arguments will ensue among the attendees as sides are taken, usually on matters that have nothing to do with the purpose of the meeting.

When you send out the meeting announcement you should only invite those that really need to be in attendance. If your invitee list exceeds four or five persons, then you need to rethink why you are calling the meeting or what you intend to accomplish.

Attendance swells when the person you invite decides to bring three associates with them. Make it clear that you want the invitee to attend or, if it is acceptable, that the invitee designates a qualified representative to attend in that person's place. "I believe the five of us can reach a decision quickly" is a way of conveying that attendance is intended to be limited.

Adding that phrase conveys the impression that a

decision will be made and that whomever attends from the invitee's area must have the authority to make a decision. There is no bigger waste of time than to spend 45 minutes debating a situation to arrive at a conclusion and then the persons in attendance are not authorized to make a decision. If someone is authorized to make a decision but will not make it, you may need to read the chapter on Murder by Memo for a solution to this problem.

The meeting invite should establish who will be the meeting leader. Meetings have a tendency to disintegrate when it is not clear who is in charge. Keep in mind that the most senior person in the room does not automatically become the leader. If you request a meeting that you will not attend but your subordinate will, you must make it clear that your subordinate is running the meeting. There is the possibility the meeting leader is the least senior person in the room. If you are the senior person at a meeting you did not arrange, show respect to the person in charge. Do not try to take over the meeting, even if it is offered to you.

In your meeting invite, it is critical to announce the purpose of the meeting. This can be handled by briefly announcing what the purpose is and providing an agenda. Suggesting a meeting without a purpose or an agenda does not guarantee a poor meeting, but it is not recommended. Providing a purpose and an agenda prior to the meeting allows the persons in charge of affected areas to know what level of expertise is required to compliment the meeting. Time prior to the meeting can be spent preparing the proper presentation for their area of expertise.

You have decided there is no need to prepare an agenda – wrong! In order to control the meeting, you need an agenda, a well thought-out agenda. Meetings are usually called to resolve problems. You should be fully aware of what the problem is. You do not need to know what the solution is. If you did, there would be no need in having the meeting. If you have decided what the solution is, send everyone an e-mail detailing your solution and not have a meeting.

Providing an agenda at the start of the meeting gives everyone an opportunity to review it while you are trying to conduct the meeting. Some participants may ignore what is being discussed until their area of concern is being discussed. Others may try to take over the meeting by immediately discussing their area. Neither situation is helpful. Providing an agenda to everyone before the meeting has greater benefits than surprising the participants at the meeting.

Problems that require a meeting are typically not one problem but a series of problems. Or solving one problem can or has created another problem. You need to consider all of the present and potential problems. Within that group there is usually one problem that must be solved. If it is not solved, the rest of the process is immaterial.

Prepare a list of all the known problems that need to be addressed. Identify the one problem that must be solved and make it the first item on your agenda. You should know which invitees will be responsible for addressing each of these problems. Write their names behind each of the problems. The results of listing the names should mirror the same names that are invited to the meeting. If not, your invitee list may be incorrect.

When you sent the meeting invite, you may have copied persons higher on the chain of command. They would be welcome to come to the meeting if they wished. If you felt it was important to let them know that a meeting was taking place, you should also let them know what were the results of the meeting. This can be done by sending them a copy of the report prepared by the note taker (described below). You can also use the report to inform subordinates of the results.

One of your goals for your meeting is to keep it as short as possible. Having the agenda and identifying key problems beforehand helps to accomplish this goal. Other factors can be worked into your meeting to assist you in keeping the time commitment to a minimum.

Have coffee and water in the room. People will only need to leave if they need the restroom. Have paper and writing instruments available in case someone forgot to bring those items. Make it known that participants should leave their mobile phones in their offices or at least turned off. Schedule your meeting shortly before lunch or normal dismissal time. And most importantly, be prepared yourself.

Having a meeting should not be an opportunity to try to blindside someone. Setting someone up to be embarrassed will be recognized by the other participants. You will lose political capital. If you feel that someone may not be adequately prepared, send that person an e-mail before the meeting. Outline the problem where you are expecting them to take the lead during the discussion. They are given the opportunity to prepare themselves.

Possibly the most important part of the meeting is the designated note taker. Assign this task to someone or yourself. Experience will dictate who are good note takers and reporters. The key is taking the notes AND reporting the results of the meeting to all of the participants. There is nothing worse than 4 people leaving a room and thinking four different decisions were made. The note taker must prepare a report that is sent to all participants so everyone knows what final outcome was decided.

Unfortunately, it is not unusual to get directed by senior management to organize a meeting on very short notice. You will not have time to do all of the niceties described above. Experience will enable you to cover the main points mentally. Identify the problem, limit the number of people invited, invite decision makers, have an agenda, take notes and distribute the report.

Meetings are essential to the continued operation of a company. Handled properly and with forethought, not only will you enjoy success but gain respect from your peers and superiors.

The Decision Tree

An axiom that I shared with my employees on a recurring basis was: if you are doing your task the same way that you did it two years ago, there is a chance you are doing it incorrectly. Individual and departmental processes need to evolve. If your product changed, if a new product was added, if new technology is available for making an improvement, if senior management's priorities changed, then decisions regarding when and how to implement the changes need to be made. Following the proper processes will facilitate making the correct decisions.

New ideas come from three main sources: senior management, your employees, and yourself. When presented with a new idea, there is a decision-making process that you need to follow. This decision-making process needs to be followed because even when you receive a directive from senior management their directive may have been made on insufficient or incorrect information. You need to go through the following steps and advise senior management if you feel that they are making a mistake. I would suggest you have all of your research done and facts readily available if you find it necessary to challenge senior management's decision.

Your employees are great sources of information and new ideas. They are the hands-on folks. Many ideas will add no or limited value to the processes but you need to look at each one in depth. Let the source of the idea know that you looked at what was suggested. If you reject the idea, an explanation of why it is being rejected needs to be shared with the employee who presented the idea. Failure to do this will eventually shut off future ideas from your employees. When an idea is worthy of implementing, let all of the staff know who presented the idea and that you are moving forward with it. You are the judge of all new ideas from your staff. Be sure to let them know what the decision was and why.

You are the third source of new ideas. You should know all of the processes that fall in your area of responsibility. You should know the strengths and weaknesses of the process. It is not unusual that the weaknesses of a process are secondary to the current environment when the process was developed. When the environment changes, take the time to revisit processes. Keep in mind that a change in senior management or even your supervisor is a change in environment. An idea that was rejected in the past may now be viewed favorably.

The decision-making process revolves around four key questions, in the following order. Is the change good for the company? Is it good for the customer? Is it good for your people? Is it good for you?

Our company had an outbound telephone unit that completed data missing from applications for insurance. This unit consisted of over 100 people and made over 20,000 calls per week. Here are three scenarios where the decision-making processes were followed. Do we make phone calls on Sunday's? Do we make phone calls on Saturday's? Do we make phone calls on Friday nights?

Determining if the change is good for the company is usually fairly simple. If your idea adds $50 of expense and increases profits by $500, then it is probably a good idea for the company. Looking at the three scenarios above, making phone calls that complete applications produces more issued policies which results in increased premium income. The immediate conclusion would be that each scenario benefits the company.

Making phone calls on Saturdays gives us the opportunity to reach folks that are not available during the week due to jobs, school, etc. That is good for the company. The same applies to making calls on Sundays and Friday nights so it looks like full steam ahead.

Testing phone calls on Sunday was very short lived. We made 5 contacts and 3 of them voiced their displeasure for being contacted on a Sunday. They requested we cancel their applications. While we were successful on 2 of the calls, the loss of the business on the other 3 was not good for the company. The quick decision to stop calls on Sunday was not difficult.

Testing phone calls on a Friday night showed people were receptive to us calling. However, our contact rate per hour dropped dramatically. Even with the reduced number of completions, it was still profitable for the company.

Calling on Friday nights is good for the company but is it good for the customer? We did not run into any objections from customers about being contacted on Friday night. We shut off all attempts to contact a customer after 9:00 PM their local time. Contact rates were down as people were out to dinner, basketball or football games, movies, parties, etc. Those people likely did not know we tried to contact them so there was no kickback from them. Calling on Friday nights is good for the company and good for the customer.

We determined that the decision to call on Friday nights was not good for our people. What did our people want to do on Friday night? Participate in one of the activities our customers who were not at home were enjoying. Secondly, our people were compensated by the number of completions they were able to obtain. I don't recall the exact numbers but it seems like an employee completing 6 calls per hour was making $18 per hour. When that contact rate dropped to 2 or 3 calls per hour on a Friday night, their pay dropped to $6 to $9 per hour. Calling on Friday nights was not good for the employees so the practice was stopped.

We have already determined that calling on Saturday is good for the company. Because we catch people at home that we do not catch during the week, it is good for the customer. How about our people? Contact rates on a Saturday were not as good as it was during a week evening. But it was still high enough that our people could make a decent hourly wage. Testing showed that calling in the morning had better results than calling in the afternoon. Afternoon results looked a lot like Friday night's activity. We missed people who went out of town for the weekend, went to their kid's soccer game, or were on the golf course. These are activities that our own people like to do. So what to do? Good for the company, good for the customer, good for some employees. We made Saturday calling completely voluntary.

If it is good for the company, good for the customer, good for your people, and good for you, it is probably a good decision. You will notice that good for you has not been discussed. And the reason for that is if the company, customer and your people are all winners, that makes you an automatic winner. Making a decision that benefits you only is a true loser. And I can assure you that all employees will recognize that type decision for what it is.

Good decision making is not hard if you follow the simple rules described above. And if your decision is challenged, you have the necessary facts to support your actions.

Controlled Failure

C orporations have goals, divisions have goals, departments have goals, you have goals. Goals are easy to establish. Sometimes these goals may be in conflict, making them difficult if not impossible to achieve. You are put in the position of failing and there may be little you can do. The key is recognizing what is causing the failure and learning how to control it.

Senior management may decide to control costs by requiring you to staff for the low point of production instead of employing the necessary personnel to handle peak periods of production. You will fail on a recurring basis, depending when peak production is required, unless you do something to control it.

Overtime is usually the easiest solution to implement for the understaffing potential failure mentioned above. Some of your people will love it; others will hate it. If your peak production time is once or twice a month, this is probably the best solution because your people will not get worn out and you can usually predict when the peak production period occurs.

If peak production happens during each week, overtime may not be the best solution. The cost of the overtime may exceed the cost of adding additional staff. The additional salary cost may defeat the savings originally projected from your staffing levels. Further, your employees may get burned out and disengage from work which also may decrease performance and attendance.

Another choice to solve the likely failure is to do staff shifting. Within your operation find tasks that are not critical for producing the required output. Train the people who are doing those tasks to perform other tasks that are critical to output. If you need an additional four people on critical days, borrow those people from within your own department. You will fail in the areas where the minor production is being ignored but you are controlling the likely larger failure.

We received over 50% of our weekly mail on Monday morning. Our goal was to have all of the Monday, Tuesday and Wednesday mail opened and scanned for data entry by Wednesday evening. We had 3 people on staff whose primary responsibility was to open the mail. On Monday we would add 2 people to that staff from another area. Depending on volume, we would work overtime on Monday and Tuesday to accomplish our goal.

It appeared that our labor costs had gone up to accomplish our goal. However, labor costs did not increase. It was not unusual for our regular mail openers to get Friday's mail done by noon. They were able to go home and the overtime costs disappeared.

Another possibility to attempt to solve a potential failure is to look at other departments around you. They may be operating under the same staff restrictions as your area. They may have the same peak production issues as your department but a different time. Borrow people from their departments during your peak times and loan people to them when they are needed.

The solution to potential failure may not reside in assigning more people to the task. There was a period where we had five mail openers and would bring in additional people to help. And even with overtime, we still failed on a recurring basis. We needed to make the processes more efficient. Two approaches were implemented – automation and production reports.

Our letter opening equipment was not very effective. It had a tendency to be slow and would cut the documents inside the envelop. Some of the cuts caused us to have to call the people to get clarification of what was put on their application. Every year or so, we would check with vendors to see if there had been any improvement in the equipment. It took time but we found a letter opener that would open the top of the envelop at the rate of about 500 letters per minute. It did not cut the contents. It cost over $10,000. Our corporate philosophy was a new piece of equipment should pay for itself in labor or material savings within two years. As the new letter opener no longer cut the documents, we were able to pay for the equipment through labor and lost sales savings within 6 weeks.

Individual production reports are critical. We were having production issues because our staff was not performing at an expected level. I did not know this until I had a means of measuring the performance of the staff as a whole and as individuals. After doing some standardizing assessments of what a reasonable production level should be, the individual production reports were compared to the standard. It showed that some personnel were not performing at acceptable levels. The employees were counseled, given refresher training, and given a deadline to increase their production to acceptable levels. Two of the people left the department.

Refresher training is important for all employees, regardless of length of service with the company or in their current position. This training obviously needs to include what processes they need to follow. What is commonly overlooked is a refresher of exactly why the task they are performing is so important. There is no magic timetable as to when refresher training needs to take place. A helpful hint is to review the individual production reports to determine if an employee or the entire department has started to slide from past levels of performance.

If there has been any change in the processes or if a new product has been introduced, the standards need to be revisited. Even if there has been no change, the standards need to be retested at least yearly. This will reaffirm to you that your standards are reasonable and will defuse any defensive feedback from under performing employees. Small changes can have a large impact. Making the paper smaller or larger, changing the color, altering the orientation of a stack of paper – all can have an impact on production. Do not take changes for granted and be sure to explain to the employees why any change was made.

There are usually two sources of failure – senior management and you. Senior management may establish goals for you that are unreasonable. This could be based on ignorance, inaccurate information from other sources, misperception of what it takes to complete a task, or direction to them from executive management. If the goals are unreasonable and you do nothing about it, you now own the failure.

Keep in mind that the person giving you the directive may have a white hat (see chapter 1) Confronting the issue has to be handled delicately. But if you have details of your staff's production reports and the results of several standardized assessments, you can show that a 50% increase in production cannot be done with the current staff. Facts have no emotion and you need to keep the conversation on a fact basis. If the facts give you no relief from the expectations, you just need to grin and bear it.

There is one other option available to you. Note the area of your operation that has drawn the most attention of senior management. Focus on that and prioritize where you will fail doing the balance of the process. If there is one particular product out of multiple products that seems to be of most interest, then change the process so the top product of interest gets processed first. Maybe no one will notice that the other products are lagging. But if and when they do, have your standardization assessments and production reports on hand to show the facts.

It is always nice to know when there will be a bump or a lag in production. Become friends with whomever provides input to your processes. They can give you a heads up when there is going to be a surge in production if you have not already heard it from other sources. Position yourself and your department to be able to help either your upline or downline department if they get overwhelmed with activity. After all, you are all working for the same company and it is in all of your best interests for the company to succeed.

Communication & Vocabulary

I t is obvious you want to be successful. What you should realize is your success in many instances rests upon your employees being successful. Their chances of success largely will be dependent upon proper communication from you. The root cause and therefore the resulting success of communication is a well-understood vocabulary.

A brief discussion of communication in general is appropriate prior to addressing the core topic of vocabulary. No matter how good your vocabulary may be, if proper communication guidelines are not followed, you may not enjoy success.

Written and oral communication make up the bulk of the methods of presenting ideas and suggestions to the intended recipient. Written communication is a formal means of conveying your point. It can be used to communicate one-on-one or to a predetermined group of individuals.

When composing one-on-one written communication, a common error is your assumption that the communication will only reside with the recipient. As mentioned elsewhere in this book, written communication is like a gift; once given you have no control over where it may eventually be re-gifted.

A second error when writing is to express an opinion. In written communication it is safer to only state facts. Attempting to support something as fact with the qualifier "Joe Supervisor told me this" is not a good strategy. Prefacing your fact with "it is my understanding" may not necessarily add more credence to your fact but does not appear to disgrace a fellow employee. Stating opinions can be dangerous as opinions may be based on only half the story. If you do not have sufficient time or resources to confirm what appears to be a fact, then the "it is my understanding" phrase becomes critical if the fact is not true. You may be criticized for not confirming the fact but will avoid the criticism of making a bold false statement. Repeated statements of unconfirmed facts may earn you a black hat (see the chapter on White Hat, Grey Hat, Black Hat).

The third error commonly made is assuming that the more you write the more you know. Some topics are not easy to explain and require extensive detail. The way to escape that is to ensure that your opening paragraph of no more than three or four sentences condenses what you are trying to say. The following paragraphs can then provide the details that support the opening paragraph. Rule of thumb is that if you cannot make your point within the first paragraph, you probably do not have one.

The final error to be discussed should never happen. And if it does, there is a good chance there will be adverse consequences. Never accuse anyone, by name or by department, of being the source of a problem that you are discussing. Error number one above, you never know where your written communication will be sent, and error number 2, you may not know the whole story, which may end up haunting you. If in fact another person or department is the cause of a problem, you may have an opportunity to voice that opinion in subsequent communications. Hopefully someone senior to you will ask for that perspective from you. At that time you can make an "it is my understanding" opinion fairly safely.

Written communication to a larger audience needs to avoid the pitfalls described above. For additional insight, please review the chapter in this book entitled "E-Mail Etiquette".

Verbal communication takes two forms and there are some minor rules for both. There is verbal communication when you initiate the contact and when you received unannounced contact.

When doing face-to-face verbal communication you are initiating, you know what the topic is. Anticipate what questions or objections you may encounter and have the necessary data or company rules at hand to address those inquiries. If the conversation may be confrontational, be sure to have a witness. Be prepared to address attempts to either change the subject or to focus on a minor portion of the discussion. It may be beneficial to prepare an outline of what needs to be discussed to ensure that all important points are covered.

If you have been called to a meeting where you know you will need to provide input, try to determine before-hand the nature of the primary topic and prepare for it just as you would if you were initiating the contact.

The phone rings or there is a knock on your work-space door. Someone wants to have a conversation with you regarding a topic for which you may not be prepared to discuss. It is critical you keep the conversation to the facts. And it is acceptable to preface your statements with "it is my understanding". Do not express an opinion. And if you are asked a question you are unable to answer, it is acceptable to respond you do not know the answer but will find out and get back to the person with the information.

I had a situation where I thought I had the answer but did not properly think it through. The Chairman of the Board and the President called me to ask about some expense items. They were pricing a new product. Did I know what it cost for a medical exam and blood chemistry test to qualify for life insurance? I had seen the invoice earlier that day and responded with the costs for the exam and the nurse's charge to draw the blood. I felt pretty good about it. The Chairman had never called me before and I was able to respond to his inquiry. My good feeling quickly collapsed. I found a separate invoice from the laboratory that analyzed the blood specimen. I had given the wrong numbers. The next morning I conveyed the correct numbers to our President. The Chairman never called me again. And I learned to say "I do not know" when I was not absolutely certain.

The core topic of vocabulary brings to mind another chapter in this book: I Do Not Know What You Know. It discusses the potential downfalls of not knowing what your employees know. There is a worse scenario: when you think you know what your vocabulary represents and you are wrong. If you say "apples" and think you are saying "apples" but the recipient thinks you are saying "oranges", your best plan of communication often gets distorted.

When cramming for industry tests regarding areas where I did not do a lot of work, the most successful technique for me was to spend a couple of hours reading the glossary at the back of the book. This sure beat the hours necessary to read the entire text and actually learn why and how the processes should work. With this minimal expenditure of effort, I was usually able to muddle through the multiple choice questions and figure out what the answer should be.

In essence, I learned a brief overview of the "what" vocabulary but skipped the "why" and "how" meaning of a particular term. I had enough to survive a two hour examination but to go deeper into the topic was not reasonable nor necessary.

Your employees need to know the what, why and how of your vocabulary in order for them to be successful. If they do not know the what of your vocabulary, the why and how may not fall into place. The question then becomes what do you need to do to ensure that the employees understand and have the same vocabulary as you do?

The apparent quickest and easiest solution is to create your own glossary. Recalling the preparation for an industry test, this approach will be highly effective for about two hours. The real value of creating a glossary is threefold: it will make you stop and think as to what words are really critical to the operation of your area, remind you of what those words mean to you, and provide reference materials for your employees that will actually use it. This effort will probably benefit you more than your employees.

There is a solution for new employees and a separate solution for existing employees. I will address new employees first.

Prepare a list of important terms for your area without definition. Give the list to new employees and ask them to complete the definition in their own words. An expectation of three new words being defined each day would be reasonable. The definitions should be recorded in writing by the new employees. Schedule a time for the employee to come to you to discuss the three newly defined terms. It may only take ten minutes of your time but it does two things: it ensures that the employees are learning the correct definition of the terms pertinent to their new position and the employees are given confidence you are taking steps to ensure they are successful in their new responsibilities. With a sound foundation of the "what" vocabulary, the "why" and "how" will follow.

Existing employees require a different approach.

First of all, they will probably consider any exercise such as noted above as silly. Secondly, they are currently being overworked and do not have time to comply with your request. And thirdly, they already know all that they need to know.

Do not give the entire list of terms that you provided to the new employee. Present two, three or four terms to existing employees, preferably in writing. You need to retain a copy so you can keep track of the terms distributed. While it is best for the new employee to write their definitions of the terms, verbal discussions with existing employees may be sufficient.

You may be surprised to learn that the employees have a different understanding of the terms you use compared to your understanding. Misunderstandings can lead to errors, usually recurring errors.

Feel free to modify this approach to fit your own environment. The potential for benefit is very real. The worst case is that at least you will identify employees who will or will not buy in to new approaches. I would recommend that you repeat this process with existing employees every two years. They can fall into bad habits or be influenced by outside sources which may literally change their definitions of key terms.

One final item for the new employee is a list that needs to be distributed on the very first day. It is a reference list of people. Depending on the size of your business or the efficiency of your HR Department, the new employee will learn at some point the key people in the organization and what areas fall in one's area of responsibility. You may not realize it but it is in your best interest if you provide your new employee with a list of names of people she may encounter personally or via other communication. Even if they may never meet the CEO, they need to know who the CEO is. If your immediate supervisor meets your new employee and her name is not recognizable to the employee, it reflects poorly on you.

If the identification of key personnel is a task normally handled by HR, I would suggest you ensure your new employee has that list. And take a few minutes to highlight personnel you deem critical to your area's operation for the new employee. It will make your life and the life of your new employee more comfortable.

In conclusion, communication and vocabulary are areas where you have complete control.

The unexpected phone call is the most difficult to handle. Trying to please by giving an opinion is dangerous. Trying to show how smart you are by having an answer to every question is fine but only if you do have every answer.

Initiating a phone call or a face-to-face conversation is like preparing for a meeting. You need to have an agenda, either written or mental, to ensure you use the proper vocabulary and process.

Your written communication may end up anywhere within your corporate structure. I always tried to review my writing from the standpoint of "would my Mother understand this?". If not, I would review it again before sending.

Communication and vocabulary – the keys to success. Handled properly, your communication will demonstrate up and down the chain of command you are in charge and know what you are doing. You have to work at it every day. A positive impression can be lost very quickly with one poorly constructed e-mail, memo, or phone call.

I Do Not Know
What You Know

In the course of doing business, you are going to hire new employees. Whether it is a new employee related to the growth of your area or a replacement of a departed employee, a new base of knowledge is being added to your staff. If the new member is a transfer from another department or a promotion within your department, you cannot become complacent and presume that the new addition knows all you think she knows. You must take the position that you do not know what your new employee knows.

A concept that was introduced to me in a management class was called the Man/Job overlay. When you hire a new employee for a position, you obviously need to know the skills set required to be successful.

"Wow, I hired this person that fits all of the criteria required for the position" is probably a bad decision. If you hire a person that can perform all of the tasks required of the position, you have hired someone that is ready for promotion. You may need them at the current time but not for long. They are ready to move on.

You want to hire someone that can perform most of the tasks required but not all or an insufficient number of the tasks. You want to leave room for growth but not so much that they would be overwhelmed. Take two napkins. One for the job and one for the proposed employee. Overlay the proposed employee napkin onto the job napkin. If the proposed employee napkin completely covers the job napkin or does not cover enough of the napkin, do not hire that person.

It is a good visual to use when explaining to your superior or to Human Resources why you did not hire a specific person. In either case, the particular details and requirements of the position may not be well known to either. Trying to explain details to persons not familiar with the processes can be a challenge.

Another aspect of the selection process is probably well known but may not be well thought out on your part. What are senior management expectations? Is the expectation this person will maintain or return activity to previous results? Or is there an expectation of seeing an improvement in results?

If you ask senior management, the answer you will get is there is an expectation of improvement. However, that may not be the case. If the position is open because of promotion, retirement, or business expansion, this would suggest there is a level of satisfaction with the current results. If termination or demotion was involved, better results going forward are expected. Use the expectation level when deciding how much of the Man napkin needs to overlay the Job napkin.

You now have a new hire on board. You have your first conversation as immediate supervisor. What do you talk about? The normal rah-rah stuff, glad to have you on board, looking forward to working with you, etc. And then you announce the basis of the relationship. I do not know what you know. Therefore, in order to have the same baseline, I am assuming that you know everything that I know. It sounds harsh.

Obviously, you know the employee's knowledge base is not equal to yours. If it is, then you hired the wrong person. There are various ways to elevate the new person's knowledge to the same level of knowledge as yours. But here are what I consider the two most important: getting rid of baggage and confirming their vocabulary.

Whether the new person came from another

company, another department, your department or just graduated from college or the military (the worst kind), there is a baseline of misconceived ideas. This is the baggage. You have to get rid of the thought process the person brought from their previous environment. This is not an easy task. In all cases you need to emphasize there is an established way that things are done here and the employee needs to learn what those processes are.

If the new person is from another company, do not automatically be dismissive of what the new person has to say. "Well, we did it this way at XYZ Corporation." It is an opportunity to address internal issues that you are having and asking how those types of issues were addressed at XYZ Corporation. You may learn something.

If the person is from another department, their knowledge of the new area is probably based on grapevine information and biased opinions from their previous supervisors. Listen and you may learn something about your own area.

The biggest mistake can happen when you promote someone from within your department to a new position. The tendency is to change their desk but not explain the changes in their responsibilities. Working under the assumption that because they had direct interaction with the new position, they know everything that needs to be done is an error. A strong discussion regarding their new responsibilities must be conducted – probably on more than one occasion.

Convincing them to let go of their previous responsibilities is also a challenge. They believe they were promoted because they were the best anyone could be at their previous job and no one is really qualified to fill their old position. This is the baggage that needs to disappear.

And the final group – college graduates and military - both came from black and white environments; there was no gray. College students have most of their experiences from books. Books and real world do not always have a very close relationship. Military are from a yes and no chain of command. If it is yes, I do it; if no, I do not – not a lot of middle ground. Teaching either of these groups is a challenge and in some cases you may never successfully rid the employee of all of their baggage. It is a combination of adding knowledge and changing attitudes.

The second approach of importance is ensuring your employee knows your vocabulary. Words have meaning, but not necessarily the same meaning among companies or even among departments within a company. Establishing a vocabulary that can be used and understood by all within the department is imperative. Trying to standardize a vocabulary within a company usually occurs though usage. Vocabulary is important to the extent that there is a whole chapter in this book devoted to that topic. Please read it.

So here is the last part of the conversation you need to have with your new employee. "I do not know what you know. I assume you know everything that I know. I will continue to operate under this premise while I elevate you to the proper level. When I get rid of your baggage and ensure you have the proper vocabulary, you will know everything that I know. Knowledge breeds success. Any questions?"

Why Things Do Not Get Done

Your people have their normal tasks that they do every day. There are expectations as to how much work is to be done. There is also a level of quality that is expected. Special projects can be assigned, usually with a timeline. Unfortunately, there are times when you are disappointed with the results. Sometimes daily tasks miss their goals on a recurring basis. You need to examine the three reasons why things do not get done.

Subordinate Reason #1: I do not have enough time to perform the task.

This could be a legitimate statement. The key is whether it stands up to closer examination.

If daily results are not meeting the goals of the department, the last item to look at is the level of staffing. That comes after further investigation of several other areas.

Exactly what are your people doing? The devil is in the details. Look at the process step by step, making sure that each step is being done correctly. You may be amazed at how people visualize a task and determine that extra steps are required to successfully perform what is requested. If extra steps have been inserted in the process, not only do you need to remove those steps but you need to go back to ensure that those steps were not started again after you left. Old habits are hard to break.

Is each step being done correctly? There are two potential problems: the people are not doing their job correctly or the procedures are flawed. Each possibility needs to be examined.

Does the step really need to be done? Here is where you need to be really careful. You must have a full understanding of the whole system, even in areas that are not under your supervision. A step that looks like a waste of time may be crucial further down the road in the whole process. If you eliminate a step that results in the next step or the next department having a product that is unworkable, you have not saved anything. You actually may have made things worse. On the other hand, "we have always done it this way" is not a good reason to continue it.

Does the step need to be done at this time or even in this area? You need to be both forward and backward looking. If you are at the start of the process, does it make sense to do what you are doing now or is it better that this step be performed later in the process? A lot of this depends on the skill sets required to do the step. It is not unusual that at the start of the process the skill sets requirements are at their lowest. Does the expertise required to perform the step match the people who are doing it? This becomes really important in the middle of the process. You want to ensure that your higher skilled people are not performing lower skilled tasks.

Are the tasks being prioritized properly? Multiple tasks may be performed by the same people. The examination of which tasks are done first is discussed in greater detail in the chapter on Controlled Failure.

After successfully addressing all of the items above, the last item that needs to be addressed is staffing. Determining the level of staffing is really quite easy. First of all, determine the average number of hours of work you have each week. And then how many people do you need to do that work. So 2,000 hours of work each week would require 50 people working 40 hours a week. So you need 50 people. Wrong. Present that number to senior management and you will be in trouble. With holidays, vacation, sick days, it would not be unusual for an employee to miss 5 weeks of work per year. The amount of time missed could be more, depending upon your company's policy on vacation, sick time and holidays. In this example, you would need approximately 55 people to cover the 2,000 hours of work.

And how much work will you actually get out of an hour of labor? Bathroom breaks, coffee breaks, cigarette breaks, personal phone calls – could be as much as a 15% loss of productivity. That would move your staffing requirements up to approximately 63 people to perform 2,000 hours of work. You need to take all of these factors into account when calculating your staffing needs.

Based on the numbers you can make your presentation to senior management. You have done all of your analysis of the process to make it as efficient as possible. You show them the math. Good luck because you probably will not get what you requested. If you find yourself in this situation, then it is time to read the chapter on Controlled Failure.

Subordinate Reason #2: I do not know how to do it.

It is human nature that if there is a task that is difficult or impossible to complete from the perspective of the worker, they either do not do it, delegate it to someone else, or put the lowest priority on the task. If one of those choices is being made, these employees may not have the skill sets necessary to do the job. Or they have not been provided the proper training.

Before you try to determine why they do not know how to do it, you need to know how to do the job. Having a conversation with employees where they are the smartest person in the room regarding the task is not a good situation. Your proposed solution to the problem may not be well received. Or worse yet, your solution ends up being a total failure.

If you have multiple areas of responsibility and multiple tasks, it may not be possible for you to know how each task is performed. If that is the case, there is nothing embarrassing about consulting an expert who does know all of the nuts and bolts of the process to assist you in your discussion. These behaviors actually make you look more committed to resolving the issue.

It should be a frank discussion; a discussion of give and take. You (or your expert) are not there to lecture. You are there to obtain the appropriate information to resolve the situation.

If it is a training issue, then prepare a plan to address that issue. The worker will be able to report back to his co-workers that you are interested in what he does and how he does it. Not preparing a plan and sharing it with the worker is a mistake. Preparing a plan and then not implementing it is an even bigger mistake.

If there is a lack of skills which training will not fix, the solution is obvious. This person needs to be removed from the position and potentially from the company. It may be that this person should never have been hired for this position. Or the person has been with the company for a long period of time and the task has evolved beyond his skills level. In either case, call in the experts from Human Resources to address the changes that need to be made.

Subordinate Reason #3: I do not want to do it.

The simple solution to this is to show this employee the door. If you do not want to do it, fine. I will find someone who will. That is the knee jerk reaction and may be correct.

The company has made an investment in this person. You want to salvage the company's investment if at all possible. You need to visit the items discussed above. Have the requirements of the task evolved beyond their skill sets? Is the person properly trained in completing the task? Does the process need to be changed? And the one question that is seldom addressed – does the person know why this task is important?

When these questions are adequately addressed and answered, then the solution is usually apparent. Again, you may need to call upon Human Resources if the solution is that they are better off somewhere else in the company or just somewhere else.

Processes are correct, staffing is adequate, training is proper, right people for the right job – all needs to be addressed when things do not get done. Remember: a happy employee is a productive employee.

Change in Your Pocket

The concept of *Change in Your Pocket* is not my invention. I was exposed to the principal over 30 years ago in a management class. I have had the interim time to see how it works.

When you were hired by the company, both you and the company had high expectations. This was a start to or continuation in your career. You evaluated the company and decided that it was the place for you. The company had done likewise before selecting you over the other candidates competing for the position.

What you may not realize is that you started your new job with change in your pocket. You had a credit balance in your account. It was up to you through your performance to impact that balance.

Of course, if you are the son-in-law of the

Chairman of the Board, your pockets are over flowing with change. But that can be adjusted, too. When the Chairman retires, you will be on your own.

Before you fully learn the culture of the company or the preferences, work habits, and characteristics of your peers and superiors, you will make mistakes. Initially these mistakes will be viewed as newcomer mistakes and they will not cost you a lot of change. But as the newness wears off, recurring mistakes likely result in change being taken out of your pocket.

So how do you lose change in your pocket? Most of the ways are fairly obvious but need to be repeated. Forget to show up for a meeting. Show up late for a meeting. Come to a meeting unprepared. Fail to support your supervisor where he will be embarrassed in front of his peers or superiors. This failure could be to contradict your supervisor in a meeting or not bring him up to speed on a project that will be discussed.

The list can go on and on. There seems to be one underlying factor that creates all of these situations. Your attitude. You decide what attitude you bring to the job every day. A bad attitude will usually produce bad results.

So how do you add change to your pocket? You come up with a new process that saves several steps - the Company saves money and you get more change put into your pocket. Consistently preparing accurate reports on time can get you more change. If work flow is backed up, be willing to do tasks below your grade level to get the work done adds change. If necessary, working overtime without being asked increases your change account. Note that a good attitude can produce these results.

Work accomplishments are not the only manner in which employees can add change to their pockets. Volunteer to take charge of your department's United Way campaign or similar project. Even if it really is not your thing, go to the company Christmas Party. If the company schedules a weekend service project for charity, be sure to attend. If you have the opportunity to have a social meal with senior management, be sure to take it. One of our senior officers once said that it is difficult to get angry at someone once you have had a cordial evening of breaking bread together.

Not all of your superiors will view your pocket change the same way. Your immediate supervisor will put in and take away change on a regular basis. That person should be your primary emphasis as he has the greatest impact on your career.

Persons higher up the corporate ladder will have a different perspective regarding how much change you have. A lot will depend upon how much interaction you have with them. If they recognize your name but do not recognize you on the elevator, then their primary source for your account balance is the people directly below them.

The up side of senior management having an impact on your account balance is that they can put large amounts in your pocket. Of course, the downside is that they can take most or all of your change in one fell swoop. Once senior management starts to take change out of your pocket, they will rarely put it back, even if deserved.

If there is a major failure that is connected to you, senior management may direct that you be fired. However, if you have enough change in your pocket, your supervisor may step up and protect you. If you do not have much change in your pocket or your actions cause your supervisor to lose considerable change from her pocket, your supervisor will help you leave.

I had a person who did not have enough time to perform one of the required tasks of the position. The fact that she did not have enough time was primarily my fault, not hers. Failure to perform that task resulted in numerous persons acquiring excessive amounts of life insurance coverage. There were over 150 persons with far more coverage than we intended to allow. Senior management suggested that this person be terminated, but she had a lot of change in her pocket. I suspected that most of the over insured folks had purchased the coverage but had no intent on keeping it.

So, I took a chance and instead of termination, transferred her to another area of responsibility. The inventory of the over insured, through attrition, gradually reduced to about 12 cases. The bulk of the risk had been avoided and I kept an employee that was able to provide value to the company.

To the best of my knowledge, that person is still with the company and adding value.

Your immediate supervisor does not control how much change you have in your pocket. You do. Here is a true-life example.

I had an employee of 20 plus years of service. She did her work faithfully and accurately. If overtime was required, there was never an issue with her staying as long as needed. The problem was that she had trouble showing up on time. She started spending the change in her pocket.

I changed her starting hours from 7:30 AM to 8:00 AM. That worked for about three days and then her arrival time slipped to 8:10 and then to 8:15 AM – she was spending more pocket change.

I changed her starting time to 9:00 AM. That worked for almost two weeks before 9:10 to 9:15 became the norm. More change was spent. This person was getting pretty low on change.

Because the time of the day did not seem to be

the determining factor to her punctuality, I changed the start time back to 7:30. It did not take long. About a week later, she came in at 7:32 AM. By 7:45 AM she was gone.

People suggested that dismissal due to being late two minutes seemed to be harsh. The explanation – all of her change was gone. She had nothing left to pay for the discretion.

Take the time to analyze what you need to do to increase the change in your pocket. It will be time well spent.

Keep in mind that those folks with the most change in their pockets are the ones who get promoted.

Errors

Things go wrong. Expected results are not achieved. Embarrassment, frustration, loss of stature within the company can all be realized when errors occur. On close examination there really are only two types of errors: errors of process and errors of judgment. It is important to know which type of error occurred in order to take effective corrective action. The bad news is that on final analysis, the most common culprit for these errors is you.

Before each error is discussed, it is imperative to visit reporting. While I am not going to go into great detail of the reporting process itself, it is absolutely a must that you develop effective reporting on what is transpiring in your area of responsibility. You need to know you are getting the expected results. If senior management, through their reporting, is required to point out to you that you are not achieving the desired results, visions of achieving a white hat have become much dimmer. If you come to work at 8:00 AM, by 8:30 you should know what, if anything, did not work properly the day before. If you do not know, then you better revisit your reporting.

What is meant by errors of process? It means that the instructions, guidelines or practices related to performing a task are either flawed or are not being followed. System issues and people issues – either or both can play a role in not achieving the results expected.

Determining if processes are flawed is the first step in examining the problem. And the action you take is dependent upon your position in the overall process. There are four possible positions: the beginning, the middle, the end, and the whole process. As the middle is often the most difficult, the bulk of the discussion will center on that area. The same principles apply to the other three positions.

Being in the middle means that your area is receiving work products from someone else and after your work efforts, the work products are being passed along to another area. So the very first question that needs to be asked: are the work products your area is receiving in the proper form for your processes to work. If your processes needs to receive X, Y, and Z but you only receive X and Y or you receive X,Y,Z and D, there are opportunities for errors.

You need to have some controls in place to identify if the products you are receiving are the products you expect. Those exceptions need to error out somewhere during your process so a supervisor can determine if the flawed product can be allowed to proceed. Not every error should stop the whole process. You need to determine what your area can or cannot accept.

When these exceptions are noted, they need to be brought to the attention of the manager who is feeding your area the work product. Keep a record of the number and types of exceptions with dates for your own protection. This reporting will allow you to know if the exceptions are being addressed or if the other area is sliding back into old habits.

The same applies when you are passing a partially finished work product to another area. Keeping a record of the number and types of exceptions with dates that are being reported to you from the subsequent area handling the task is critical. You need to know if your area has a recurring problem. If it does, then you need to review what happened to the corrective action you directed to have implemented to solve the problem initially.

If what you are receiving is fine, then review the fully documented procedure that pertains to your area. There is no documented procedure? Get one! It is critical to have one, as a training tool, as a reference for your supervisor, as a reference for you and your subordinates. When senior management asks "What are you doing?", you have something to share with them.

When the product that is being provided to your area changes, it is imperative to be in a position to change your procedures very quickly to handle the new requirements. Without fully documented procedures, assumptions or promises to management could come back to bite you. And if automation becomes an option, it is easier to identify where automation will work and where it will not.

Identifying who (people issue) is causing the problem can be a challenge. We had a situation that was causing huge problems in another department. One of our data files was constantly being corrupted and we could not figure out why it was happening or who was corrupting it. The problem was there were seven people who had access to the file. We cut that number down to two people. Going forward when the file was corrupted, we knew it was either employee A or employee B. We got them both in the same room and found out one of them had not been properly trained. So the problem was a result of not ensuring that the staff was trained; problem solved. And we avoided future problems by limiting the access to the file to two people going forward.

If you get a group of employees in a room and go over a procedure, everyone in the room will agree they are following the steps in the right order. You need to work with small groups if at all possible. Employees will not stand up in an auditorium and admit they were doing something incorrectly. With smaller groups, supervisors can check work or figure out a way to attach an identifier to work product that helps flesh out whom needs additional training.

Often there is a tendency to think the younger

employees need the additional training – this is not always correct. Some of the more experienced workers may rely on "we used to do it this way" and let those old procedures work their way into the current process.

While I cannot assign an accurate percentage, I concluded most errors of process committed by employees were secondary to not being properly trained. Training is time consuming and expensive as you often have to pull productive employees off their jobs to do the training. However, the time and resources spent on training, especially for new employees or new processes, most often saves time, money and energy down the road.

Unfortunately, I learned of the importance of training new employees immediately the hard way when a manager not properly trained worked six months before errors were noticed. We had enough successful transactions masking the errors. It took an additional four months to clean up the mess – and install proper reporting so it did not happen again. The cost of fixing the errors far exceeded what it would have cost to properly train this employee in the first place.

Training is not easy. See the chapter on "I Do Not Know What You Know" for further detail on the training process.

With proper reporting in place, a fully documented process and extra time spent training the employees, nothing could go wrong. Except you are dealing with people. I am having a bad day, I need to finish this so I can go on break or lunch, my husband will not pick up the kids, etc. If the primary task is mental and not physical, there is an endless list of reasons the process can get off track. Here is where the supervisor plays a vital role.

Did you take your most productive worker, promote them to supervisor, and give them 15 minutes of training? I did. Bad mistake. The work was completed in record time secondary to the efforts of the supervisor. The error rate went up, secondary to the lack of supervision. The supervisor was more interested in doing the work than in making sure everyone followed the procedure.

Customer complaints are sometimes routed through senior management. And their big picture view is not always receptive to your narrow explanation. Having an established procedure to share with management is helpful but explaining why the procedure was not followed can be challenging.

I will not tell you the secret to selecting good supervisors because I was never able to crack the code on how to do that. I am sure that there are numerous reference materials available that can guide you in your particular situation.

Whether you are front, back, middle or the whole process, there will be expectations of your area's performance. It is important to know who set the expectations. If you set the expectations and you are unable to achieve the projected results, use your documented procedures and reporting to show senior management that you over shot the mark. But your procedures and reporting better be air tight.

If senior management sets the expectations, then an analysis of the basis for those expectations is imperative. Was it because you improperly communicated something to senior management? Did you throw out a number to try to impress them? If you did, good luck. If not, then you can survive.

At one point, senior management gave me a goal that appeared to me to be unachievable. We were at 65% of applications received resulting in policies being issued and senior management thought the activity should be at 75%. The 75% was based on opinion and not on fact. Each percentage point meant an additional $1 million in profit for the company each year. The process was reviewed and modifications were made to attempt to meet this goal while at the same time not impacting the risk taken by the company. The end result was that we moved the percentage to 72% but could go no further. Proper documentation and reporting supported that this was the best we could do.

Errors of judgment means what? As the name implies, a judgmental decision was required and the wrong decision was made. The most common situation that results in an error of judgment is when resources or time are insufficient. So a decision has to be made as to how and where to allocate resources to the best effect. (See the chapter on Planned Failure.)

Several questions need to be asked and answered before the error can be properly rectified.

Question Number 1: Who had the authority to make the decision? As the responsibility for the area begins with you, only you have the authority to make the decision. You can delegate that authority to your supervisors or even your line people but you cannot delegate responsibility.

Question Number 2: If you delegated the responsibility to others, do they have the proper training to make the decision? From your experience you often can itemize the typical problems that occur. From that you can derive the best decision and share those problems and decisions with the person delegated to make the decision. As part of the training process, you will also provide procedures for the delegated person to follow when problems outside of those described occur. The delegated person should never be in a position of "what should I do?".

Question Number 3: If your procedure is for the delegated authority (including yourself) to consult with someone prior to making a decision, is it clear what the situations are that require consultation and whom should be consulted? If a supervisor is coming to you and asking what to do because the printers are out of ink, then you have not done your job. If the printers are out of ink and none will be available until tomorrow causing part of your process to cease, the supervisor needs to know to make you aware of the situation. And most important, you need to be aware of the situations where your immediate supervisor wants to be part of the decision process.

Question Number 4: Is there a contact procedure if the party to be consulted is not available? The printers are out of ink, you are not available, and the supervisor contacts someone in senior management or worse, does nothing. Neither of those scenarios will play out well for you.

Question number 5: When you have had a bad result from a decision, are the results discussed with the decision maker in a constructive way? Prior to your discussion, you need to review questions 1 through 4 first. Then you can have a meaningful discussion and try to improve on the process.

Errors in process usually have no basis for defense. You typically cannot argue your way out of those. Errors in judgment are more fluid and can have a basis for discussion. If you have done your preparation work properly, at least you will have something to discuss when senior management decides to reproach you for either type of error.

The Dumb-Tough Rule

The Dumb-Tough Rule was shared with me by a co-worker several years ago. He was a former football coach. In this extremely physical sport, he advocated that "if you are going to be dumb, you better be tough". While this advice was directed to football players, it applies to many other areas – especially in the business world.

Businesses, like football, engage in competition. They use a variety of techniques designed to give them an advantage over competitors. Some techniques are fair; others are not. The business pages of newspapers/magazines and various other sources (e.g. information on the internet) periodically detail unfair practices that step over the line. These stories often summarize what they did and how they were caught.

On a much smaller scale, unfair practices may be going on in your work environment. Determining if such practices are occurring needs to be a priority for you. To ignore the possibility, you might be dumb. If unfair practices are in play and you do not know it, you need to be tough.

The best approach is to determine the attitude of your supervisors towards you. Your actions likely are what created the existing attitude. Only a direct approach can resolve any potential issues.

Discuss with your supervisor what actions created a poor impression of you for them. You do not need to acknowledge that any of those actions are a reflection of what you do. Your supervisor may have wanted to mention these actions to you but either did not want the confrontation or to embarrass you. Ask what steps you need to take to not aggravate your supervisor. Do not be dumb.

If you are in a position where people report to you, be sure that you share the following with your people: It is important to tell them what turns you off. What turns you off is more important than what turns you on, because many turn ons will be overwhelmed by one significant turn off. Unreturned phone calls, long e-mails, missed deadlines, tardiness for meetings, are some of the examples. Your supervisors will typically share with you what really hacks them off.

If your supervisors are reluctant to share with you information regarding what turns them off, pay attention to them especially when they talk about other employees. Criticisms of their superiors, their peer group, or your peer group are clear clues as to what aggravates them. Remember, an aggravated supervisor is not a happy supervisor. They may be in a position to take action that will reflect poorly on you. If they do, prepare to be tough.

Also, be aware of the people higher on the organizational chart that have an influence over your career. Some of those will be people who would not recognize you on the elevator. Your only method of impressing them is through your supervisor. If your supervisor likes you and/or your work, you will be properly represented to this level of supervision. If not, you do not have much control over that situation. Options are to live with it, transfer to a different supervisor, or get a new job.

If your supervisor's superior has a casual relationship with you, then you have the opportunity to impress him with your work. But you have to be careful as to how you handle it.

Do not go around your supervisor to present ideas or work products to your supervisor's superior. That would be dumb. If the superior asks you to perform a specific task, be sure to keep your supervisor informed of what was asked, the deadline imposed, and the results of your efforts. If you have questions that need to be answered in order to accomplish the task, do not direct those questions to the superior. Rather, route those requests through your supervisor. If your request is dumb, it is better for your supervisor to know it than the superior. If your request is really dumb and your supervisor passes it along to the superior, then your supervisor is not on your side or will also look dumb. You will both need to be tough.

Keep in mind that part of your job description is to ensure that your supervisor is never embarrassed (because of you). There is nothing worse than your supervisor being questioned at a meeting about a project you are working on that your supervisor knows nothing about. It is almost guaranteed you will be exposed to the down side of the Dumb Tough Rule after the meeting.

Your professional future with your current company is closely linked to the relationship that you have up and down the corporate hierarchy. Confirming where you stand with those persons on either side of your level of authority and being aware of their needs are big steps in helping you move up the hierarchy. To do otherwise would be dumb. And if you are going to be dumb, you better be tough.

Little Victories

I was in Dublin, Ireland setting up the administration of a new company. Dealing with the Home Office of our parent company and the Central Bank of Ireland presented many challenges that I had not been exposed to previously. Below I describe two of these challenges that illustrate how little victories can be vital to your psychic well being. It is important to recognize them when you have them. And more importantly enjoy them and share them with your co-workers. It may help them notice little victories of their own.

I recorded in a diary some of the events that transpired while I was in Dublin. While some of this is not pertinent to the title of this chapter, to try to edit it and abridge it does not seem to be the appropriate approach.

The two topics that are being addressed are the first life insurance test that I took and getting a communications switch from America. I only took one test out of six to obtain my QFA (Qualified Financial Advisor) required by the Central Bank. I passed with 55%. The second was dealing with Federal Express, customs, and the folks who sent the package to me.

Here was my take on Little Victories.

Sent: Sat, September 3, 2011 10:24:09 AM
Subject: Number 18 - Little Victories

Everyone wants to hit a home run or score the winning touchdown or shoot a hole in one. That thrill only comes to the few – and talent is not always a factor in who gets to enjoy that thrill. So instead you need to strive for little victories. Not necessarily noticed by anyone but you but moments when the defeats and frustrations of the past seem to become less important.

Sometimes you have to stretch your imagination to create a little victory in your own mind. But that is ok. The end result is what is important.

So this was a week of little victories. First of all a big worry has gone away. I took my test early this afternoon – and in my mind, I passed. A little victory. We will have to see what the grader has to say. Tom, our Irish employee, took me in his car on Thursday to find the test site. Decided on my best path to get there. And on Thursday, I went by myself to find the place.

Took the tram to the Harcourt station and then walked about

a mile and a half to the west, or what I think is the west. Found the campus of Griffith College, which I am told is a converted World War II barracks, and the building that I was to go to. No one was around and there were no signs so presumed it was the place. Another little victory.

Left this morning around 11:00 AM and actually got to the building around 11:45. There were people and there were signs indicating that I was at the right place. Little victory.

Had taken a practice test earlier in the week, had finished in about an hour and had scored a 71%, 50% is passing. Little victory. Was going to take it again but decided that if I scored better that would be a boost and if I did worse, I would start to question my original 71%. Decided to leave 71% as a little victory.

They pointed out at the start of the test that there were 80 questions (just like the practice test); 3 points for every correct answer, minus one point for every wrong answer, and fill in option E on the multiple response test sheet if you didn't want to answer (no points). Oops, my confidence in my 71% started slipping as I didn't know how many of those I got right were because of guessing.

I usually like to start tests in the middle and work backwards from there. Turned arbitrarily to question 44 – I know this answer. Attitude on the mend. Question 43 – are you sure this is a question from our book? I have never heard of this before. Attitude sliding, which can be bad during a test.

Went to the front of the test and ended up finishing in about an hour and 15 minutes – we had an hour and a half. Ended up filling in option E on 9 questions so I only have 71 questions on which to get potential credit. I need 120 points to pass. If I got 50 right and 21 wrong, that would give me plus 150 points and minus 21 points for a total of 129. I don't think I got 21 wrong. But I will know in about three weeks.

You were assigned a number and a desk for the test. I was number 114 and I saw a guy sitting at desk 130. About a third of the desks were empty so suspect those folks decided to not fail in person. The exam costs about $400 so was really surprised that that many did not show up.

Last Friday I got an e-mail from Federal Express stating that they had a package for me but needed to know if it was VAT registered. VAT – Value Added Tax – is like a State sales tax. For most things it is 21%. I had no idea what was in the package or what VAT registered was. Answered the e-mail and questioned the folks in McKinney.

Finally found out Monday that the package is a switch that we need for our communications cabinet so we can wire phones and other devices through the firewall. I am picking up an IT vocabulary that could make me a threat at Scrabble. McKinney had no idea if it was registered or not.

Fed Ex said that if we didn't get it resolved by this Friday, they would ship the item back to the States. So the pressure is on. Went to the website and found out we needed an EORI number. I don't remember what EORI stands for – Economic something or other. Website had a form that we could complete and e-mail to them – little victory. Started to fill out the form and it started to ask questions like, do your items typically come by boat or airplane? It is a small package. If by boat, is it driven off the boat or is it hauled off?

This looks like a form for a regular importer of truckloads of goods. Tom was in the office on Wednesday. I usually understand about 85% of what is said to me by the Irish, but only about 70% when on the phone. Tom called the Fed Ex office for about 4 minutes, another 3 minutes to the Revenue office, I sent them an e-mail, we got our response in ten minutes which I forwarded to Fed Ex and they forwarded to customs who released our package. Got the switch yesterday. Little victory.

Anyway will finish today with the grocery list of the items I picked up in the store.

Two bottles, California white wine (imported, no less)	$15.00
Half a loaf of bread (no preservatives so bread molds quickly)	$2.00
6 eggs	$2.45
BBQ Pringles potato chips (can)	$3.75
Microwave popcorn (3 bags)	$2.40
Hamburger – 4 patties	$3.00
Rashers – back bacon, half a pound	$3.75

Not much else for now. If you managed to wade through all of this, give yourself a little victory.

Sam

Little victories are important – not only to you but to others. When your employees have a little victory, be sure to point it out to them. It does not have to be a big presentation in front of a large group, although if that opportunity arises, do not let it pass by. Rather, merely commenting on the little victory or a quick e-mail to highlight the victory is likely sufficient to bolster your employee's confidence and self-esteem.

The more meaningful little victories are those that are recognized by the individual and their supervisor. The special hands on attention that the supervisor provides makes for prideful discussion with co-workers, spouse, or friends. These one-on- one little victories give the recipient the opportunity to embellish on what actually occurred.

That never happens. Or have you over celebrated one of your little victories?

Murder by Memo

Murder by memo was a concept conceived before there were personal computers. Back in the good old days all communication to multiple recipients was handled through the memo process. The concept is the same; the method of distribution has changed. Instead of sending a piece of paper, the typical means of communication currently is by e-mail.

Murder by memo is exactly what the term implies; you intend to perpetuate harm on a proposed idea, or person, or even a department. As the legal system suggests, there are varying degrees of murder. The guidelines that need to be followed are primarily the same across the board. There are slight differences as the level of murder increases. These differences will be discussed later.

All of the following assumes you have done your normal management approach to issues or problems. Part of that process is determining if you are dealing with someone who has a White Hat. Be sure to read the chapter on White Hat, Grey Hat, Black Hat before reading further. If there is a White Hat involved, murder by memo may still be necessary but there likely is an added element of risk.

Attempted murder is when you want to make management aware that an area out of your control is interfering in your department's goals. If you are not receiving products prepared correctly for your department or not receiving them in a timely manner, then attempted murder is warranted. If you are properly and timely passing the product on to the next department but the desired results are not being realized, a memo is necessary.

As an example, the correspondence department is supposed to provide you letters already inserted into envelopes. You consistently get letters without envelopes, or they are inserted incorrectly, or the address does not line up with the window, or they are not kept in the same order as they were printed. These types of errors may compromise your operation. Your task is to insert individual specific information, maybe a refund check. The time and effort to accomplish this will be expanded because of the quality of the product you receive. The mail then goes to the mail room to be sealed, postage applied, and delivered to the post office. Instead of the three-day turn around from start to finish, promised by senior management to the customer, the mail room sits on the mail for three days before getting it out the door. Management may look to your area when customer complaints are brought to their attention.

Usually there is one person in either area that is causing the problem, either the worker or the worker's supervisor. The workers are not doing their jobs for multiple possible reasons but at a minimum, the supervisor is not monitoring what his staff is doing. The supervisor is the target of your attempted murder. You do not want to kill the supervisor. However, you do want to make them aware that there was an attempt on their livelihood.

Before preparing your memo, it is important to review the chapter on E-mail Etiquette. One of those aspects is "the monkey rule". If you are having a problem, then the monkey is on your back. Do not try to monkey the problem up the chain of command.

The basic rules of the memo are fairly simple. First of all, memos go up or laterally in the chain of command, never down. In the example above, you would not direct your memo to the supervisor. It should be addressed to your counterpart, with a copy to your immediate superior and a copy to your counterpart's immediate superior. Limit the addressees to only those that need to take action. You expect action from the memo's addressee but not those you have copied.

Secondly, never use individual names in your memo. To do so makes it look like it is a personal attack. Calling out an individual may divert attention from what you are trying to accomplish. Your counterpart should be able to figure out who is the source of the problem.

Thirdly, keep the content of your memo short. State facts, not opinions. Presenting data to support your facts bolsters your argument. If possible, attach this memo to previous e-mails sent in the normal course of business where the problem was discussed but not resolved. If you do not have data or previous correspondence, then you are probably premature in taking this approach. Just because something has happened once does not mean you should overreact. Our general counsel used to tell me "Remember, one robin does not make it spring."

Lastly, leave yourself an escape. You could be wrong. Your counterpart may perceive you as being wrong or just a complainer. Statements such as "I may not have the correct information, but----" or "Based on the information that I have,------" gives the recipients an avenue to try to save face. But if you have done your homework and have the facts to support your position, the response will have to be confirmation that what you have presented is correct.

Second degree murder is when the message you want to send warrants a wider audience. Situations where it is necessary to increase the intensity do occur. One example is when you are having issues getting a new idea implemented, i.e., someone is stonewalling your idea. Or an idea being implemented was originally yours but someone else is now taking credit for it. Or your previously sent attempted murder memo was ignored.

You are starting to enter a danger zone. You need to expand your distribution list up the chain of command. Do not skip anyone. Your chances of encountering a White Hat increases but you may have to take the risk. Your facts need to be air tight. You may have to use names. The upside is this may expose you to members of senior management that are not aware of you. If your presentation is well- thought out, there may be benefits for you in the future.

First degree murder is when you need to blow the whistle on something you have determined is detrimental to the future of the company. Plan on only doing this once. There will either be great reward or great punishment.

I did it once and got lucky. The man I was reporting to had been moved from another department to his current position and had no idea what he was doing. I had two year's of experience and thought I knew everything. I complained to the CEO's son that I thought my supervisor was incompetent. The next day I was called to the CEO's office to present my case. Luck was with me. Two weeks prior we had received a death claim on a policy I had issued only two months previously. I had noted in the file that I had talked to a reinsurance underwriter about the client's condition and the underwriter agreed that the client was within our acceptable risk tolerance. I had established credibility. The CEO was receptive to what I had to tell him and my supervisor was moved back to his old position the following week.

The moral of the story: do not confide with dependents of the CEO.

To summarize, your memo must be based on fact and not opinion. Only include those people up the chain of command that need to be informed. Be thorough but careful. With this knowledge, you may recognize someone who is trying to do murder by memo to you.

www.ingramcontent.com/pod-product-compliance
Lightning Source LLC
Chambersburg PA
CBHW021848170526
45157CB00007B/2988